YOGA BREATHING

By the same authors

YOGA OVER FORTY

YOGA FOR BACKACHE

YOGA FOR BEAUTY

SEX AND YOGA

GROWING UP WITH YOGA

MICHAEL VOLIN & NANCY PHELAN

Yoga Breathing

PELHAM BOOKS

First published in Great Britain by
PELHAM BOOKS LTD
52 *Bedford Square*
*London, W.C.*1
OCTOBER 1966
SECOND IMPRESSION JULY 1972

7207 0116 3

Printed in Great Britain by Hollen Street Press Ltd at Slough and bound by James Burn at Esher, Surrey

'. . . As the lion, elephant and tiger can become tame only very gradually, so also must be treated the *vaya* (vital air); otherwise it kills the practiser.'

Hathayoga Pradipika

CONTENTS

ILLUSTRATIONS

PHOTOGRAPHS

CHAPTER ONE

Hatha yoga and breath control. The dualistic principle. Preparation for breath control. Higher and lower aspects of breathing. General ignorance of correct methods. *Prana*. The curative properties of breath.

All through history scholars and thinkers have sought the secret of life in breathing, from the Egyptian Book of the Dead, through the old Chinese Healing Breathing, to modern sanatoria in Switzerland; but only *Hatha yoga* has made a complete study of the subject.

Yoga is one of the most ancient of all philosophies. It is mentioned in the Vedas – the sacred writings of India, the oldest books in the world – but figures of yogis in meditative poses, believed to date from thousands of years before Christ, suggest it is far older.

The ultimate goal of yoga is reintegration, union of the individual soul with the soul of the universe, but this union may be sought in different ways. Varying paths make it possible for man to choose the yoga best suited to his nature and temperament. *Hatha yoga* is the path of bodily strength and control.

The name *hatha* suggests that it is intimately concerned with breathing practice. It is taught that the flow of breath through the right nostril is controlled by the sun, through the left nostril by the moon. In Sanscrit *ha* means the sun; *tha*, the moon; and *yoga*,* union. *Hatha yoga* is therefore unification of sun and moon breaths in the human body.

The sun and the moon symbolise the dualism of human nature, explored also by many mystical schools other than yoga. In varying proportions, male and female characteristics exist in all of us – the most masculine man has certain female elements, the most feminine of women possess masculine instincts. This dualistic principle is of great importance in the study of breath. The sun breath (the positive force), is identified with masculine characteristics, the moon (negative force) with feminine. The joining or union (yoga) of these breaths, achieved by numerous breathing practices and techniques, is said to produce at will a state of super-consciousness known as *samadhi*, in which the yogi passes beyond the dimensional plane of existence. In other words, unification of male and female principle, through breath control, brings complete pacification of human nature and permits liberation of the spirit . . . unification with the universe.

There are eight steps listed in the classical *Hatha* yoga treatise. These are:

yama
niyama } – observances and way of living

asana – bodily poses

pranayama – breath control

* From the Sanscrit *yuj*, to join or yoke. Refers also to the unification of the individual soul with the divine principle.

pratyahara – withdrawal of the senses from external objects
dharana – concentration
dhyana – contemplation
samadhi – identification

Control of breath is placed after the study of bodily position and immediately before mental practice, leading to spiritual enlightenment. The body must be strengthened, disciplined and purified before it is ready for serious breathing practice. This training is achieved through 84 traditional *asanas*, or bodily positions, each one a challenge to strength, agility and suppleness. Symbolically, with each *asana* mastered a rebirth is achieved.

Yoga breathing could be divided into *Low or Physical Exercises* and *Higher Practices*, for the ancient yogis knew that apart from its power in psychic and spiritual attainment, breath purifies the bloodstream; that the more complete the inhalation-exhalation the more efficient the purification, the greater the nourishment derived by vital organs, muscles, glands and nervous centres. 'One who breathes correctly stays young longer . . .' 'The body remains pure and unchanged as a mountain stream, rejuvenating itself through itself by breathing . . .' 'To breathe correctly is to live correctly . . .' – these and similar yoga proverbs emphasise the importance placed on full understanding of breath on the physical as well as spiritual plane.

The main concern of the physician, midwife or nurse assisting the birth of a child is to ensure the first breath.

When this is drawn and the first cry uttered, a new independent life has begun. Whether it lasts 100 years or one day, its entire span will be a succession of breaths. No one who has watched a first or a last breath could fail to be awed by the extraordinary change it brings . . . in one case, an inanimate piece of flesh transformed to a living being; in the other, a living being returned once more to inanimate flesh. Breath, the greatest commonplace of life, is also its greatest mystery.

We know that we can live without food for thirty days but without breath only a few minutes (divers who do so regularly pay dearly for the practice); yet, in over 30 years of teaching, the authors have met no untrained adult who knew how to breathe properly. Though more are now aware of the correct method, mainly due to the spread of yoga, and more scientists are studying the subject, the general public remains ignorant.

Most of the blame must be laid upon wrong instruction in childhood and youth. In general, it is natural for children to breathe more correctly than adults. Healthy children under five breathe in the true yoga manner; but bad methods, for so long taught in kindergartens, schools, training camps, soon replace the instinctive method. Until recently, in some schools, children were being taught such wrong practices as exhaling through the mouth.

Conditions of modern life, especially in big cities – overheated stuffy offices, badly-ventilated public transport – sedentary work and life also help establish incorrect and inadequate respiration, while the stresses and strains of the western world and ignorance of the art of relaxation contribute to, as well as derive from, bad breathing habits.

Apart from the physiological functions of breathing, which are explained in Chapter 2, yoga teaching includes an additional and essential principle that must be understood and accepted by all students. This is the *pranic* theory.

Prana

For centuries it has been widely recognized that in certain parts of our planet . . . high mountains, pine forests, by the sea, in the fields . . . the air possesses particularly powerful, invigorating, energy-charging, even healing properties.

This extra Something is cosmic energy, life force, known in Sanscrit as *prana*. It is present in all forms of life and in all things having life (page 17). It is in the food we eat, in water, earth, sunlight, above all in the air we breathe. Since it is thus taken into the body in breathing, improved inhalation means increased supplies of life force.* The extra supplies are stored in the solar plexus – the seat of physical energy – from whence they may be directed to other parts of the system. The increase of vital energy through breathing is one of *hatha* yoga's main aims.

* We breathe normally between 15-20 times a minute. With each incoming breath *prana* is taken into the system without conscious control. Yoga teaches that we are not yet mentally or spiritually ready to completely control it, though after a certain stage of development we may learn to do so without fear.

Prana is the power that keeps the body together, preserving health, protecting us from the changes we know as ageing. It is our energy, vitality, vigour. Without adequate supplies – when vital energy is low – resistance to infection decreases; eyesight and hearing are affected; the sufferer becomes less active, consciously or unconsciously 'sparing' his muscles, which leads to their deterioration and eventual flabbiness; digestive power and metabolical processes are affected; the entire inner life of the body is thrown out of balance. When the amount of life force is high, physical activity, mental alertness, creative fertility are increased.

The balance of energy cannot be maintained by nourishment alone. There must also be correct breathing. When the method – or art – is learnt and practised regularly, physical and mental conditions are improved in a very short time and ageing delayed to a considerable extent.

Curative properties of breath

People of the west sometimes smile at the seemingly extravagant claims made in traditional yoga literature for breath as a cure-all; yet medical research is confirming an increasing number of these claims and the treatment of certain ailments by breathing is now widely practised in many countries.

Switzerland and other high mountainous areas have long been used for T.B. sanatoria because of the purity of the air – or in yoga terminology its greater amount of *prana*; but fresh air and improved breathing methods are also among the chief measures now used in Russian health centres for regeneration and the continuance of good health at every age; while China has established Breathing Clinics in which the only form of treatment for various maladies is rest and specified periods of deep breathing.

As science advances we see more and more modern scientists reaching conclusions of the ancient yogis . . . in geriatrics and delaying age, in exploring states of consciousness, in the power of the mind, in breath control. Though the word *prana* is not yet used in western science, implications are not dissimilar. Health experts now act on the belief that energy may be taken into the body from water, as from air (see pages 47–48); and the suggestion that the healthgiving properties of fresh air come from the minute electrical charges of ions parallels the yoga definition of *prana*.*

Accounts of modern public health measures in some countries read very much like yoga teaching . . . insistance on prevention rather than belated cure; the power of the mind; the importance of keeping the body fit by proper exercise; the essential need for training in correct breathing and relaxation etc.

The phrase 'Breath is life' is a cliché; yet few of us

* A typical exercise illustrating the teaching that *prana* is in all forms of life is to breathe near freshly-cut grass. Life-force is believed to be given off by the grass for some time after cutting. The same exercise may be practised walking in a pine forest, on pine-needles. The scent – of grass or pine-needles – is identified with *Prana*, in inhalation; with exhalation the life-force is transformed to bodily energy.

ever pay five minutes attention to our breathing unless illness or some emergency gives it prominence. Breath, our greatest gift, would appear to be the one we know and bother least about. In this we can learn from the ancient yogis who knew and taught that 'One who controls breath, controls life itself.'

CHAPTER TWO

The respiratory system. The process of breathing. Incorrect methods . . . shallow breathing; mouth-breathing. The physical effects of breathing. Breath and emotions.

The Respiratory System: Methods of breathing

A general idea of the structure and functions of the respiratory system is necessary to a full understanding of the value and importance of correct breathing.

This delicate and marvellous apparatus includes the *lungs*, situated in the chest, and a series of air passages connecting them with the outer air.

Entering by the *nostrils*, with inhalation, the air travels through the *nasal passages*, down through *pharynx*, *larynx*, *trachea* and *bronchi* . . . (two, left and right). Inside the lungs, the bronchi divide into smaller tubes (*bronchioles*), terminating in a honeycomb of *alveoli* or air cells containing bloodvessels. There are said to be about 700,000,000 of these air cells, which, if spread out flat would extend for thousands of feet.

The *neck*, *chest* and *abdominal muscles*, including the *diaphragm*, are also important components of the respiratory system.

The lungs are porous and spongey and are enclosed in the pleural sac. They are set one on each side of the heart, with which they work and to which they are connected by veins and arteries.

The cells of the body are fed by the bloodstream circulating through the system, driven or pumped by the heart. The blood starts its journey purified, bearing nourishment, through the arteries and capillaries; it comes back to the heart, through the veins, bringing wastes and poisons.

Before another circuit begins, the contaminated venous blood must be purified and charged with fresh oxygen for the body cells. Entering the *right auricle* of the heart it is pumped into the *right ventricle* (see Fig. I) and on into the lungs where it travels to the blood-vessels of the alveoli. Here it absorbs oxygen inhaled in breathing and releases its impurities in the form of carbonic acid gas; then, purified and oxygenated, it returns through the *left auricle* and *ventricle* of the heart to be pumped out again round the body, while the carbonic acid gas is discharged with exhalation.

If insufficient oxygen is received the blood resumes its circulation incompletely purified, carrying undischarged wastes and poisons back to the body cells, tissues, organs, muscles. This recontamination could cause disorders ranging from headache, lethargy, general lowering of health and vitality, to death.

The process of breathing

The act of inhaling and exhaling – filling and emptying the lungs with air – is carried out by the diaphragm, chest walls and floating ribs. Because the movement of the diaphragm is less obvious than that of the chest

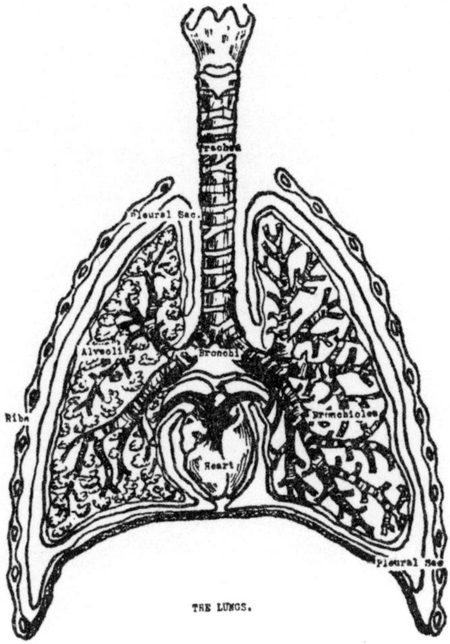

FIG. 1 Heart and lungs

walls many people are ignorant of its importance, but without it we could not breathe. When it is flattened (in inhalation) it creates a vacuum which draws air into the lungs; when it returns to normal position (in exhalation) the air is expelled.

The air entering the nose with inhalation passes through the nasal passages which are lined with fine hairs and mucous membrane full of blood-vessels. These fine hairs act as a filter, screening out dust and bacteria, while the mucous membrane warms and moistens the incoming air, preparing it for entry to the lungs. (A gulp of air taken in through the mouth on a very cold day illustrates the importance of this warming).

Having ultimately reached the alveoli, the oxygen is absorbed by the venous blood which has come there to be purified. The stale air bearing discarded wastes is then exhaled.

Incorrect breathing and yoga breathing

Shallow breathing

In most cases of so-called normal breathing, action is concentrated on the upper part of the chest. There is no conscious attempt to use the diaphragm in drawing more air into the lungs. Shallow breathing gives inadequate scope for the inhaled oxygen to permeate the alveoli blood-vessels and recharge the venous blood. The yoga diaphragmatic breath, which also involves movement of the abdomen, (see page 38), corrects this fault; while another yoga practice, retention of breath, permits the incoming fresh air to mix more efficiently with the static air in the lungs, reducing possible contamination of the system that could result.

Mouth breathing

Breathing through the mouth is injurious to health, mental alertness and appearance. If allowed to persist from childhood it may deform mouth, teeth and nose.

Since air taken in through the mouth is neither filtered nor warmed before entering the windpipe there is increased risk of infection and – frequently – constant colds.

The traditional open-mouthed village idiot is a good illustration of the connection between mental slowness, even apparent stupidity, and mouth breathing. Many normal children have been temporarily retarded through this practice. Despite our much publicised health and education programmes, yoga teachers frequently encounter adults who seem surprised to learn there is an alternative and better way of breathing.

Yoga exercises based on instinctive breaths

Breath not only purifies the blood and keeps the cells alive, it stimulates the circulation, regulates the body temperature and is closely connected with metabolism – the process by which nourishment is built up into living matter – and therefore with weight. (Checking metabolism involves 'a breathing test.')

Many yoga breathing exercises are based on everyday functions. Laughing, sobbing, coughing, sighing, talking, all involve a certain change in the breathing pattern . . . singing, reciting, public speaking particularly requiring special breath control. These instinctive changes are natural methods of purifying the blood, pacifying and resting heart and nerves, or increasing vital energy. The yoga Cleansing Breath is inspired by the act of sighing. A tired person sighs repeatedly, as though trying to rid the system of fatigue. The Cleansing Breath is an emphasised sigh of relief . . . accompanied by a consciously-formed image of tiredness expelled from the body.

The natural preliminary to increased physical exertion or sustained ordeal is to take a deep breath and hold it. This instinctive effort of the body to increase its vital energy is the principle behind the yoga Recharging Breaths, which consist of deep inhalation and retention.

Breath and the emotions

We often tend to forget the close connection between breathing and the nervous system, between breathing and the emotions. We know that agitation, rage, fear accelerate the rate of the breath (this is the body's instinctive reaction to possible emergency, preparation for escape or struggle), but many of us are not aware that the process may be consciously reversed . . . the nerves calmed, agitation or anger subdued by deliberate slowing of the breath, inhalation of *prana* and the power of the mind. In many such ways a knowledge of yoga breathing could become an inseparable and valuable part of daily life, in addition to benefiting physical health and vitality.

CHAPTER THREE

Conditions benefiting from improved breathing: Resistance to infection. Asthma. Chronic bronchitis. Emphysema. Ankylosing Spondylitis. Silicosis. Heart conditions. Before surgery. Head colds, catarrh, sinus troubles. Shortness of breath. Insomnia. Lack of appetite. Fatigue and loss of vitality. Nervous tension. Emotional disturbances and negative thoughts. Smoking.

Conditions benefiting from correct breathing

The yoga complete abdominal breath is now recognized in the West as having therapeutic powers and the method is widely used by physiotherapists. Where respiratory illness already exists it often brings relief, even in incurable conditions, not only by improving the intake and discharge of air but by permitting relaxation of the muscles concerned in respiration.

In such ailments as asthma, bronchitis and emphysema, apprehension and fear increase the distress of the actual physical condition. Since a violent struggle for breath brings instinctive panic, and the knowledge that the attacks will recur creates an ever-present fear and tension, abdominal breathing and training in complete relaxation of muscles, nerves and mind is a form of help and reassurance.

Resistance to infection, chills, etc.

Good health not only means feeling well. It should imply ability to resist infection, to withstand strains and chills.

Though weakness in individual organs contributes, many illnesses come either from the body's inability to resist invading bacteria or withstand chills and strain. This applies from sciatica to nephritis, from the common cold to tuberculosis. The basic cause of such lowered resistance is diminished vitality.

Regular practice of breathing cycles to soothe the nerves and keep the body charged with vital energy will help maintain good health. These should always be done by an open window, better still out of doors, if possible first thing in the morning.

Asthma

For some years doctors have been recommending yoga for asthmatics, not only for breathing tuition but to learn the art of relaxation. Whether the origins of asthma are nervous, emotional, allergic, seasonal or infectious the course of the attack is the same.

In normal breathing the diaphragm and chest wall muscles move downwards and outwards with inhalation and relax with exhalation. Inside the lungs, the bronchioles or small subdivisions of the bronchi, dilate with inhalation and contract with exhalation.

During an asthma attack the muscles controlling the bronchioles go into spasm. Air can get in but not out of the lungs. Feeling breathless, the sufferer tries to take in more breath, but the lungs are already distended and the effort to inhale further tenses all the muscles – including those of the upper chest and neck.

To get relief he (or she) must *exhale*, but he cannot do this if he does not know how to relax the tension or control the muscles used in exhalation. Ability to use the complete yoga breath helps relax this tension. Breathing with the abdomen not only provides an auxiliary motor for use during attacks but relieves fear and the sensation of helplessness in the struggle for breath.

A bad asthma attack is a shattering experience, even for an observer; yet often the power of the mind is the dominating force. An injection of sterile water has been known to calm panic-stricken patients who believed the needle contained a relaxing drug.

When attacks are frequent the lungs become over-distended and even the chest distorted. In growing children this could become a permanent deformity, but when it has not existed too long it could be corrected by appropriate exercise.

Asthma creates a vicious circle. Fear of recurring attacks causes tension, which in itself helps precipitate attacks; repeated attacks, with subsequent breathlessness and wheezing, encourage the sufferer to avoid exertion and physical exercise. This brings lowered health and vitality which pave the way for more frequent attacks.

The asthmatic who has learnt to combat this vicious circle with abdominal breathing and relaxation should not wait for an attack to use his knowledge. The time to practise is *between* seizures, every day, until the method becomes second nature, and the full yoga breath could be applied to such normal activities as walking and lying down. It will then be easier to stave off imminent attacks and, if there is sufficient willpower and courage, to apply the method for relief during an actual spasm.

Chronic bronchitis

Bronchitis is inflammation of the bronchial mucous membrane. It is accompanied by a distressing cough and often difficulty in breathing. When it recurs frequently the continual inflammation may result in lung damage and a chronic cough. As with asthma, repeated infection encourages habits that lower health and resistance. Breathlessness limits physical activity, often causing social and economic complications; fear of provoking coughing and choking creates nervous tension and a very shallow breathing which further reduces the powers of resistance. Relaxation and correct respiration are essential not only for increasing resistance but for minimising breathing difficulties.

Emphysema

This could be described as loss of elasticity in lung tissue, resulting in damage to the walls of the alveoli (tiny air cells). It causes a feeling of constriction in the chest, difficulty in breathing and shortness of breath in exertion.

As with other respiratory complaints, fear of further attacks, of coughing and asphyxiation encourage shallow breathing, apprehension and nervous tension, all of which aggravate the distressing symptoms.

Yoga does not cure emphysema but it can give relief through teaching relaxation and complete breathing.

Ankylosing Spondylitis

This is a form of arthritis in the upper spinal joints which may affect respiration through inhibition of chest movement.

Use of the abdomen and diaphragm compensates for this disability, ensuring adequate intake and exhalation of air. In acute conditions it could help avert lung complications.

Silicosis

A stiffening of the lung tissue caused by inhalation of injurious dust. Diaphragm breathing relieves strain and permits improved respiration, even when a certain amount of lung tissue has been destroyed.

Heart conditions

Where any kind of heart trouble exists, medical advice must be sought before attempting recharging breathing exercises. In some conditions, stimulating the circulation could be dangerous. On the other hand, pacifying breaths that slow down and rest the heart and relax muscles, nerves and mind, could only be beneficial.

Before surgery

A knowledge of yoga breathing and relaxation is a great help to surgical patients – indeed in any form of illness. In the case of thoracic surgery, special exercises are taught beforehand (see page 55), but for all operations ability to relax muscles and control respiration is beneficial. The former lessens discomfort and pain, the latter reduces risk of complications after anaesthesia. The first instruction after a general anaesthetic is always to 'take a deep breath'. During unconsciousness there is a danger of fluids collecting in the lungs and causing pneumonia.

Head colds, catarrh, sinus troubles

Many cases of chronic colds, sniffles, sinusitis and catarrh have been relieved by improved breathing.

Not only does better health bring greater resistance, but stimulated circulation and cleared nasal passages discourage infection and chills.

These complaints are common among – though not exclusive to – mouth-breathers. The change to nose-breathing brings immense improvement in health, vitality, appearance and resistance.

Certain exercises (page 52) are recommended for keeping the nasal passages clear.

Shortness of breath

It is not uncommon for those in 'normal' health to become short of breath on exertion, climbing hills, steps, etc. This suggests poor physical condition, but abdominal breathing during exertion reduces the strain on the heart and the feeling that the lungs are 'bursting'.

Insomnia

Common causes of insomnia are nervous tension, mental distress or anger, exhaustion, indigestion, all of which respond to improved respiration and the ability to discharge tension.

Those who sleep but wake unrefreshed could be suffering from lack of oxygen. They should train themselves to breathe correctly during sleep. The method is described on page 58.

Loss of appetite

Correct breathing helps improve poor appetite and digestion. Increased intake of oxygen and *prana* stimulate circulation, resulting in better working of the digestive system. The abdominal organs further benefit from the regular gentle massage provided by the movements of the diaphragm. Nervous tension, which is destructive to digestion, is released through the combination of mental concentration and abdominal breathing.

Food and liquid taken into the body need oxygenation to be fully assimilated. Poor respiration means inadequate intake of oxygen and insufficient oxygenation for digestion.

When vitality is increased the body becomes more active. This in turn improves appetite and digestion.

Fatigue. Loss of vitality

We know that the body may be constantly recharged with vitality at will, through inhaling *prana* or life force from the air round us.

When inhalation is incomplete, less *prana* is taken into the system and the body's vital energy decreases. With incomplete exhalation, poisons remain in the blood, to be carried on round the system again. Chronic fatigue is a common result.

When vital energy is low the body not only loses resistance to disease but to the force of central gravity holding us to the surface of the earth. We feel increasingly heavy, tired, lethargic, less willing to move. We want to sit or lie about; everything is too much effort. Reduced activity brings loss of muscle tone, impaired digestion, general lowering of health. If not combated by techniques for recharging vital energy, the pull of gravity shows in sagging tissues, displaced organs and other signs of premature ageing.

Nervous tension

This is one of the most destructive complaints of western life. Apart from those who have learnt the art, very few can relax without the help of tranquillizers and other sedatives, which may vary in strength but are uniform in their ultimate destructive and demoralizing effects on health and personality.

Relaxation may be taught and learnt but only practice will bring ability to completely let go and discharge all tension in muscles, nerves and mind.

The key to this exercise, known in yoga as *Savasana*, is the combined powers of mind and breath. In *Savasana*, which is in four stages, the muscles are relaxed; nervous energy withdrawn; then rhythmical breathing established to speed and support relaxation and fill the system with beneficient *prana*. In the last stage the mind is detached from normal surroundings and by power of imagination and concentration the student escapes

A typical breathing exercise. Complete exhalation

Siddhasana pose, showing position of fingers for recharging from earth

Half-lotus pose—a traditional position for breathing practice

completely into a different world, relaxing in peace and tranquillity.

Emotional disturbances. Negative thoughts

Anger, jealousy, grief, hatred, frustration and all other destructive emotions may be controlled by breathing. Even simple nervousness, shyness, 'stage-fright' will respond to the change of vibrations brought about by slow rhythmical inhaling-exhaling, accompanied by a conscious effort to calm the mind. As the heart slows, in response to the reduced breathing rate, the agitation or nervousness gradually decreases. Even in obstinate cases it will be greatly relieved, while in others it completely vanishes.

Traffic blocks, traffic lights, other mechanical obstructions over which we have no control offer excellent opportunities for practising mastery of impatience, frustration, agitation. Instead of wasting vital energy in anger, concentrate upon full abdominal breathing, timing about six heartbeats for inhalation, six for exhalation.

When stronger, more destructive emotions and thought are involved, a greater effort of will must be added to the rhythmical breathing. If they have been allowed to become second nature it may be necessary to persevere for some time; but they may be eradicated if the will is present and practice is maintained. (See *Concentration on Bramahcakra.*)*

* Alternative name for Sahasrara – 1000-petalled lotus – the highest *cakra*.

Smoking

Many people, at last aware of the dangers of smoking, are anxious to give it up. If they have smoked for many years this will be very hard to do, but will-power, aided by yoga breathing, has frequently brought success.

There are no really successful artificial cures for smoking. Mixtures and pills that claim to take all the hard work out of breaking the habit may succeed temporarily by turning the body against nicotine, but sooner or later, if occasion arises, there will be a relapse. The only sure method is to WANT to give up and have the strength to hold out until the craving has died.

General yoga practice often reduces the desire for tobacco. Smoking is often the result of nervous tension and this gradually decreases with ability to relax. At the same time improved circulation, better-functioning body and mind given an increased feeling of well-being which also works against the need for tobacco.

Try to set aside a few minutes every day for fighting the habit. Sit crosslegged in the open or where you can inhale fresh air, shut your eyes and establish rhythmical breathing. (This is the prelude to all mental exercises and is the means of making the mind more receptive.) Your thoughts should be concentrated on enjoyment of the fresh air you are inhaling, and on the delicate lung tissue, so easily damaged.

Next, try to persuade yourself to give up smoking for three days. These three days – not really so long – will be difficult but are the most important in breaking the hold of the drug.

At the end of the three days, remind yourself how unpleasant they were and how foolish to have endured them just in order to smoke again. Remind yourself continually of the unpleasant aspects of smoking . . . lung cancer, surgery, etc. Finally ask yourself, who is the master – You? or the Smoking? Are you enslaved by a habit that could kill or maim you? Of a drug that destroys your will-power?

Continue to practise breathing cycles all the time you are fighting the habit. They will increase your resistance and reduce the craving. But the key to final victory is your will-power and your own strength of character.

CHAPTER FOUR

Breathing practices – physical. Breathing in yoga training. The complete yoga breath. Recharging cycles. Recharging from the elements. Pacifying cycles. Purifying and Cleansing breaths. Cooling and Warming Breaths. Slowing the heart. Breathing with one lung. Emotional control. Lying-down breathing. *Surya Namaskar* (Greeting to the Rising Sun).

Breathing practices. Physical

It has already been mentioned that methods of yoga breath control fall into two main groups . . . *Low*, or *Physical Techniques*, for invigorating, recharging, pacifying, purifying, cleansing, warming and cooling the body; and *Higher* or *Mental Methods* that affect the mind, stimulate nervous centres, act as healing agents, develop higher faculties and lead to the achievement of occult powers and *samadhi*, a trance-like state associated with experience on a higher plane of consciousness.

Although this chapter is concerned with physical aspects of breath control, a certain amount of mergence between lower and higher methods is inevitable – as in pacifying exercises and healing breaths.

Lower or physical methods could be practised in or

out of doors, while standing, sitting, walking or lying; even, in certain cases, floating in the water.

Outdoor practice should be in a secluded place, not in strong wind or strong sunshine, unless for some particular purpose such as recharging with energy from the elements. For indoor practice a well-ventilated room without draughts is required.

Physical yoga breathing could be divided into *Recharging, Pacifying, Cooling and Warming* Breaths.

Recharging techniques are designed to increase vital force in the human body.

The principle behind them is the belief – perhaps one day to become accepted by science – that man could tap his individual energy to the energy of the universe through the medium of breathing. During recharging exercises increased inhalation increases intake of *prana*; appropriate effort of will-power directs and stores this force; during exhalation – (during retention, in some techniques) – the actual separation of *prana* from the rest of the air is effected.

In *Pacifying techniques* the objective is a general reduction of tempo in the whole system . . . calming nerves, relaxing tension, slowing down the heart, stilling the mind.

Healing Breaths (see Chapter 5) for self-application or to others may be practised by close contact or at a distance.

The complete yoga breath

No breathing exercises can be attempted – nor any yoga practice undertaken – until the complete yoga breath has been mastered.

This method of breathing involves the use of abdomen and diaphragm. It permits the lungs to be filled with each inhalation and emptied with each exhalation, reducing the amount of residual air to a minimum. The technique of retaining the inhaled breath gives maximum opportunity for the incoming fresh air to purify the bloodstream.

Put the hands lightly on the abdomen, with finger-tips touching. Inhale through the nose and at the same time let the abdomen come out slowly, rather as a frog inflates in breathing. The finger-tips should move apart as the abdomen swells out.

Exhale, through the nose, at the same time drawing the stomach in so that the fingertips come together again.

Practise these movements until they are familiar enough to be performed without conscious direction. You could practise lying on your back; in the Pose of a Frog (sitting back on heels, toes together, knees apart, hands clasped over the head); – or sitting crosslegged. Pose of a Frog has the advantage that the position of the arms prevents the shoulder-raising typical in shallow breathing.

As the stomach comes forward with inhalation, the diaphragm is lowered and the bottom of the lungs starts to fill with air. As the breath continues, the lower part of the chest is expanded and the lungs further filled; finally the upper ribs are expanded and slightly lifted so that the top of the lungs is filled.

In exhalation, the process is reversed. The drawn-in stomach lifts the diaphragm, beginning the emptying of the lungs, and as the expanded ribs relax to normal position the exhalation is completed.

Thus described, the breath is in three stages, but in practice it becomes one smooth continuous movement.

Yoga breathing is performed at a slower rate than normal . . . approximately six heart-beats inhalation, six exhalation (5/6 breaths per minute instead of 15/20). You can soon learn to time yourself by practising with a finger on the pulse.

This is the purely mechanical process of yoga breathing and is the simplest part to learn. Far more difficult is the mental aspect which must also be mastered, for the mind is always harder to discipline. It is through the power of concentration that *prana* is separated from the air and directed through or to different parts of the body.

Posture is important for proper respiration. In all yoga training it is stressed that head and spine must be in one straight line with shoulders relaxed and stomach held in.

Recharging

Solar plexus methods. The solar plexus, located in the abdominal cavity just under the breast-bone, is considered to be the storage-place of physical energy in the human body. (A blow in the solar plexus is more devastating to a boxer than any other assault, snapping his energy.)

In the following two cycles, after the complete yoga breath has been inhaled, it is retained by closing the glottis – as though swallowing. During retention, the mind should be concentrated on the solar plexus, and while exhaling, an image evoked of life force stored there.

The exercises are performed standing. It is usual to combine such Recharging exercises in cycles of 7, 14 or 21 breaths, with a Cleansing Breath between each cycle.

Vigorous Recharging Cycle

Inhale through the nose, exhale through the mouth

1. Inhale a full breath, stretching arms forward, parallel, to shoulder level. While retaining breath, vigorously swing them apart to the sides, together in front, apart to sides, together, apart, together. Exhale and drop arms by sides.

2. Inhale. Retain breath and vigorously swing the arms forwards and up over the head, down, up, down, up, down. Exhale and relax.

3. Inhale. Lock the breath (closing the glottis) and swing arms like windmills, twice forward and upward, crossing in front of the chest, then reverse the movement, bringing them downward, crossing in front of the chest. Exhale and relax.

4. Inhale. Stretch arms forward, retaining breath, then pull them back against the shoulders, shaking whole body; stretch forward, pull back, forward, back. Exhale.

5. Inhale. Bend upper body to left, vigorously swinging arms up from sides to cross over the head, then down; then the same movement to the right. Exhale.

6. Inhale. Retaining breath, vigorously massage and slightly squeeze the floating ribs with the palms. Exhale.

7. Inhale, retain breath. Exhale, gently tapping the chest with the fingers. Finish the cycle with a cleansing breath. (Page 50.)

Quiet Recharging Cycle

Inhale and exhale through the nose

1. Inhale till lungs are full. Retain breath as long as comfortable, then exhale, concentrating on sending *prana* to the solar plexus and on the thought that you are breathing out only stale air.

2. Inhale. Retain breath, tensing every muscle of the body. Relax and exhale, directing *prana* to the solar plexus.

3. Inhale. Retaining breath, rise up on the toes, holding position as long as comfortable. Exhale, sending *prana* to the solar plexus.

4. Inhale. Raise the arms forward, parallel, and clench the fists as though holding a rod. Breath is retained. Then exhale, sending *prana* to solar plexus.

5. Inhale. Raise the arms and put palms together over the head. Hold position while retaining breath; then exhale, directing *prana* to solar plexus.

6. Inhale. Retaining breath, press the palms together in attitude of prayer, in front of the chest. Exhale, lowering arms and directing *prana* to solar plexus.

7. Inhale. Raise arms over head, joining palms as in

(5); then, still retaining breath, slowly lower them into position of prayer, as in (6). Exhale, directing *prana* to solar plexus, and lower the arms.

Exercises practised on the floor

Inhale and exhale through the nose

1. Lie on the back and stretch the arms over the head. Inhale, retaining breath, stretching and fully extending arms while you tense the whole body. Exhale and relax.

2. With arms by the sides, inhale and raise the chest only, arching the spine. Exhale and relax. (Good exercise to develop breathing capacity of the chest.)

3. With arms by the sides, inhale and raise the hips only, arching the spine and keeping heels and shoulders on the floor. Exhale and relax.

4. Inhale and draw the knees up, pressing them against the stomach (actually the solar plexus) with the hands. Exhale and lower legs.

This exercise (which is also practised to relieve flatulence) is not advisable in cases of high blood-pressure since it builds up pressure in the head – flushing face and head with blood. For this reason it is used as a rejuvenating and beautifying exercise.

5. Inhale. Draw the knees up, as above, but not using hands; stretch legs up straight at right angles to the body; exhale, slowly lowering them to the floor.

6. With hands under the neck, inhale and lift the body half-way into sitting position. Retain pose and breath for a few seconds; then lie down and exhale.

7. Lying on the back with hands under neck. Inhale

and lift both legs . . . keeping them straight. Exhale and relax.

Breath of Circulating Life Force

It is taught that *prana*, after passing through the nervous channels, escapes from the body, to a certain extent, through the fingertips, back into the atmosphere.* In this and the following recharging exercises the circuit is closed by the position of the fingers.

Sit on the floor with legs stretched and close together. Hook the index fingers round the big toes and interlock the thumbs. Press the chin to the chest and inhale and exhale deeply and rhythmically. The mind should be concentrated on the thought of *prana* flowing from the fingertips to the feet and legs, circulating within the body.

Solar plexus breath

In this exercise the fingertips are placed lightly on the solar plexus, and the mind concentrates upon the image of life force – said to be golden in colour – directed to this centre of energy. Practise lying on the back, either with the legs stretched or loosely crossed and drawn up. Breathing is deep and rhythmical. *Prana* is taken in with inhalation, with exhalation sent to the solar plexus.

Breathing away tiredness

This is also practised lying on the back, with legs stretched. Slow rhythmical breath is established and

* In ancient drawings *prana* is sometimes shown radiating from the fingertips as rays of light. This belief in the vital powers of the human hand is found in many cultures . . . for example, touching by the king as a cure for disease; or the laying on of hands as a blessing.

the mind concentrates upon taking in *prana* with inhalation and with exhalation sending it out through the pores of the skin, driving out the impurities in the body which are causing the fatigue. (The yoga belief is that tiredness is caused by impurities accumulated in the system).

Breathing through the bones

It is useless to attempt these somewhat unorthodox (to the western mind) methods unless there is complete acceptance of the existance of *prana* and the teaching that it could be directed at will to any part of the body.

Lying on the back, completely relaxed, establish rhythmical breathing and try to "see" life force entering the body through the bones of the legs, arms, spine, ribs, skull, etc. At first you might try concentrating on each part in turn, gradually proceeding to the whole body. As you exhale, direct the *prana* to the bones. It is important, and a great help, to create the visual image of the bones through which *prana* is being drawn.

Directing prana to the spine

Lying completely relaxed, on the back, inhale deeply and with exhalation send *prana* to the roots of the spinal nerves. Full concentration brings a sensation of warmth and refreshment.

Great physical breath of a yogi

In this recharging technique, breaths are directed to the

four most vital parts of the body . . . head, heart, spine and stomach.

The exercise is practised in standing position with feet together, breathing in and out through the nose. The power of the technique lies in the combined retention of breath and mental concentration on the four bodily parts to be benefited.

1. Standing with the palms flat on top of the head, fingers laced together, inhale a full breath. Retain the breath while stretching the arms up (palms turned upward, fingers still interlaced) and concentrating upon sending *prana* to the head. Exhale and lower the arms.

2. With fingers interlaced, place the palms on the chest. Inhale, stretching the arms forward (palms turned outward and away from the body), fingers still interlaced. Concentrate on directing *prana* to the heart. Exhale and relax.

3. With interlaced fingers, hold the hands loosely, at arms length, in the front of the body. Inhale; turn the palms downward, fingers still laced, and direct *prana* to the stomach. Exhale and relax.

4. With hands behind the back, fingers interlaced. Inhale; stretch arms downward, turning palms towards the ground, and directing *prana* to the spine. Exhale and relax.

Recharging from the elements

As well as being taken into the body through the lungs in breathing, vital energy is also drawn from the elements of earth, sun and water.

Since the yogi believes that his body is but another

manifestation of the universe around him, a different vessel to contain the life force animating all creation, he can, by the power of concentration and breath control, supplement his own vital energy by transferring life force from the elements to his body.

These practices demand full concentration. In the technique of recharging from the sun (one of the oldest in hatha yoga), as practised in some eastern *ashrams*, the yogi sits on a sun stone . . . a flat circular stone set on an upright base . . . while another disciple turns it about 90 degrees every few minutes, so the whole body is gradually exposed to the sun's rays.

Recharging from the Sun

In modern practice this may be done sitting crosslegged facing the sun, wearing the minimum of clothing. With deep and rhythmical breathing established, concentrate on the image of solar energy entering the body with inhalation, and with exhalation being transformed into your own energy.

You should turn your body slightly every few minutes so that the whole surface of the skin receives the sun's rays. Do not look at the sun.

This technique should not be practised in intensely hot sunlight. The best time is early morning.

Recharging from the Earth

Choose a quiet place in the open where you will not be disturbed. Sit down crosslegged, in the shade, with the hands resting on the knees, thumb and index finger

FIG 2. Energy from earth

closed,* and the other fingers straight (See Fig. 2) so they are making contact with the earth. With deep and rhythmical breathing established, concentrate upon drawing energy from the earth through the fingertips as you inhale and as you exhale transfer it to your own energy. Those who cannot touch the earth with hands resting on the knees could modify the pose by stretching the arms at the sides.

Energy from the Ether or air

This is practised in the same way as Energy from the Earth but the arms are raised above the head, parallel, with palms facing. The fingers, which are literally used

* Traditional position of fingers to prevent *prana* escaping.

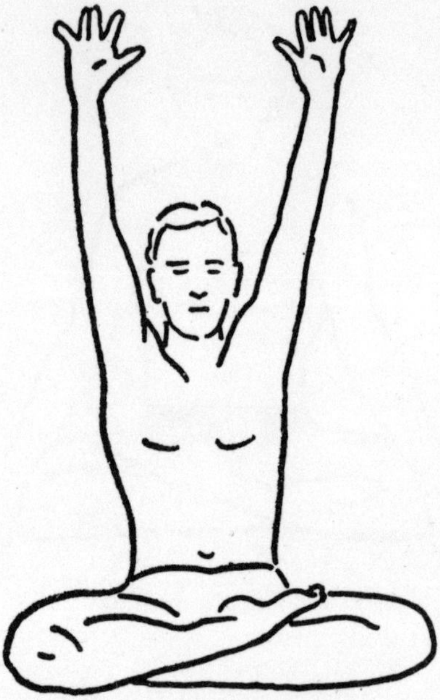

FIG. 2A Energy from air

as antennae, are spread wide and stretched straight. (See Fig. 2A).

Energy from the Water

Floating in the water, establish rhythmical breathing. With inhalation, take in energy from the water through the pores; with exhalation transfer it to yourself. If you are able to practise *Pose of a Fish* you could float in this position.

Nine pacifying breaths

This Pacifying Cycle has great power to calm the mind

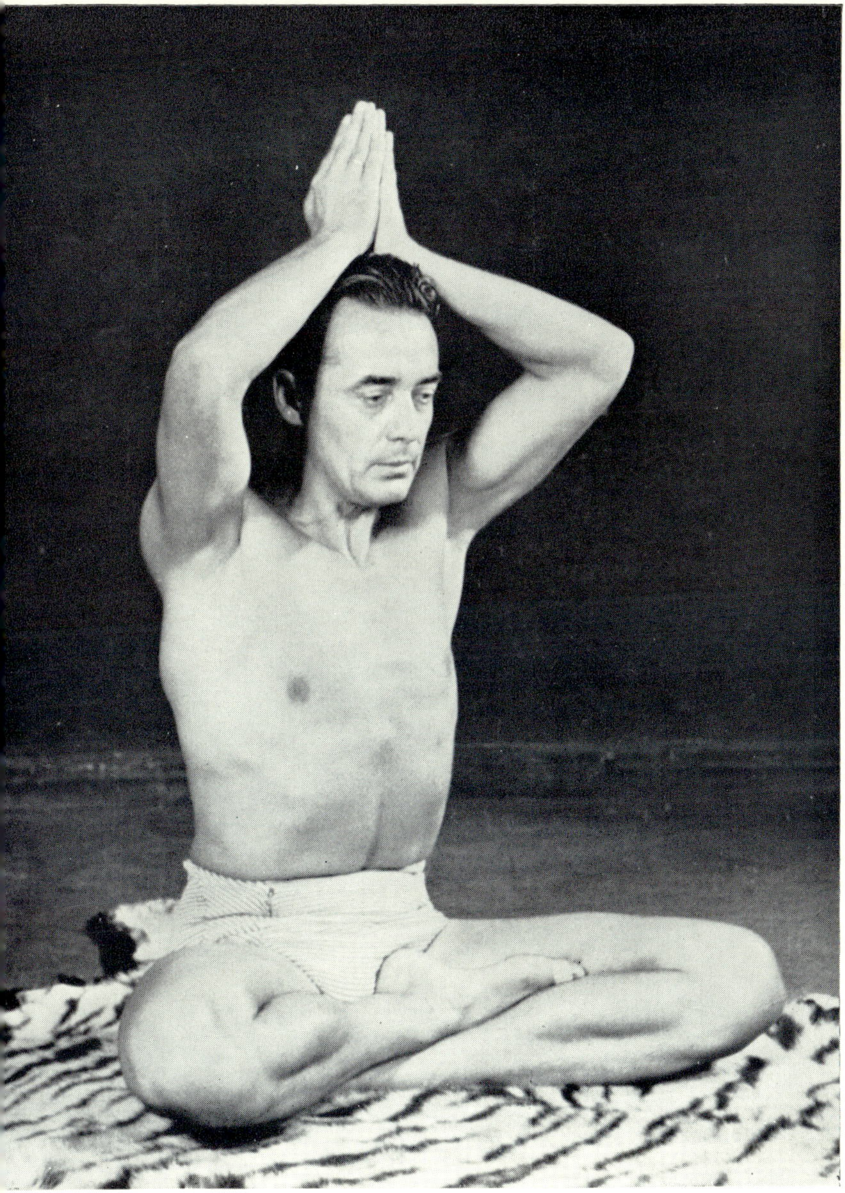

Siddhasana pose, with hands raised to facilitate abdominal breathing

Uddiyana, with Net-holding contraction

Ten-finger gesture

and relax the nervous system. It helps to improve sleep if done before an open window just before getting into bed, but is beneficial at any time of the day.

Stand with feet together, arms by the sides. Keep the eyes closed and inhale and exhale through the nose.

1. Inhale slowly and deeply, bringing the arms forward to cross in front of the body, over the head and then separate them, bringing them down to the sides again. Repeat this movement 3 times more (4 in all) with the mind concentrated on the image of a circle.

2. Inhale, raise the arms from the sides to join fingertips over the head; exhale as you lower them to the sides again. Repeat twice more (3 times in all) with mind concentrated on a triangle.

3. Inhale, raising the arms forward – parallel – over the head; exhale and lower them. Repeat once (2 in all) with mind concentrated on parallel lines.

This completes the nine breaths.

The symbolical meaning of this cycle is, Life is stronger than death. The circle represents the universe; the triangle, conception of new life; and the parallel lines, eternity – victory of life over death.

The power of the cycle is greatly increased by keeping the eyes shut.

OM Breath

Another powerful pacifying breath which is practised in one of the crosslegged sitting poses.

Breath is inhaled, retained while the mind concentrates on the sound OM, then exhaled.

If this sound can be evoked so that it vibrates through

the mind, through the whole being, the result is an extraordinary sensation of peace and serenity.

OM is sometimes used as a unit of counting or timing in *pranayama* . . . for instance, OM is repeated four times instead of counting four pulse-beats.

This exercise (OM Breath) is an instance in which physical breathing overlaps Higher practices.

Purifying Breaths

Cleansing Breaths

Shallow breathing results in a permanent excess of stale air in the lungs and this causes many of the headaches and vague indispositions, the depression, lethargy, loss of vitality that afflict the majority of modern city-dwellers.

Nature does her best for us by giving us the sigh . . . the sound so much associated with tiredness . . . which is an instinctive attempt to clean out impurities. As well as acting as a safety valve to relieve tension it is a natural cleansing breath, an effort to expel stale air from the lungs.

Indian yoga teaches two main types of Cleansing Breaths, the HA Breath and Sitting or Standing Cleansing Breath.

HA Breath

With feet apart, slowly inhale a full breath, at the same time bringing the arms up from the sides till they are above the head. Keeping the legs straight, 'throw' the upper body forward, letting the arms hand loosely, and

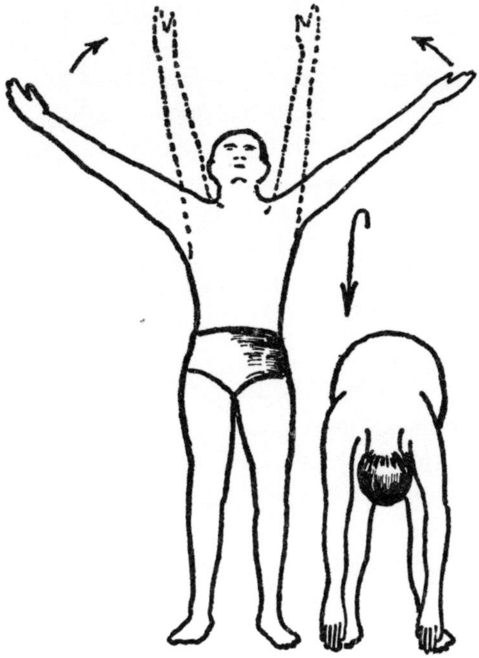

FIG. 3 HA Breath

at the same time vigorously exhale with the sound HA, driving out all the stale air and fatigue from the system. Repeat twice (3 times in all). (See Fig. 3).

Standing or Sitting Cleansing Breath

Stand with the feet together. Inhale a full breath. Make an O with the lips and exhale vigorously in short blasts, driving out stale air and tiredness by rapidly contracting floating ribs and diaphragm.

exhaling through alternative nostrils. (See page 66, Chapter 5).

Conclude the exercise by washing out the nostrils, drawing up warm salted water into the nasal passages.

Warming and Cooling breaths

Yoga teaches that since *prana* is cosmic energy it could be transformed, in the body, to the sensations of heat or cold. Advanced yogis in the East, by combined breathing and mental concentration, can make themselves completely independent of thermal changes. These are the techniques that enable them to sit in the snow, in bitter cold, not only impervious to the temperature but often actually melting the snow around them.

Though western students rarely achieve this stage, many have increased their resistance to both heat and cold, particularly the latter. Plenty of people who formerly suffered intensely from cold have trained themselves to enjoy swimming even in midwinter. There is however, little use in attempting these techniques unless there is a genuine belief in the method and a will to succeed.

Warming Breath

Sit in crosslegged position, establish rhythmical breathing and concentrate on the thought that as you inhale you take cosmic energy into the system, and as you exhale you convert it to the sensation of bodily warmth.

It is best to begin with a small area – usually the palm of the hand or one finger – trying to sense this spot becoming warmer and warmer as you continue your breathing and concentration. When you have warmed the palm, try to extend the sensation along the arm, then gradually to the whole body. You cannot expect success immediately; it requires patience, perseverence and practice. There could, however, be spectacular results . . . as in the case of the student who produced a small blister in the palm of her hand through the intensity of her concentration.

Practice need not be limited to sitting crosslegged. If you have cold feet in bed at night, try to warm them in this way; and if at any time you find yourself obliged to endure cold without a coat, apply the warming breath technique.

Cooling Breath

This is the same method, but with exhalation *prana* is transformed to the feeling of coolness. You could start by concentrating on the spine, gradually spreading the sensation throughout the body.

This is traditionally practised in crosslegged pose but could be applied in other circumstances.

Breathing through a Crow's Beak

Another cooling breath, which also has the power to appease thirst. Sitting crosslegged, with rhythmical breath established, form your mouth into a little *O*, with lips pushed forward like a bird's beak. The tip of the tongue should lie close to the lips.

Inhale through the 'crow's beak', as though sipping the air; exhale slowly through the nose. There is a slight hissing sound as you take in the air.

After several breaths the mouth becomes agreeably cool, even on the hottest day, and if breathing and concentration are continued the sensation spreads throughout the body.

Breathing with one lung; slowing the heart, etc.

A remarkable amount of control over the gross body could be developed, using the principle of *Mind is the Master* (mind over matter). Yoga is often described as the Philosophy of Complete Mastery. (The ancient proverb that a real master is not one who commands 10 thousand warriors but one who is master of himself, concisely expresses the true 'soul' of yoga). The same principle is fully recognised and successfully used in western medicine.

Ideally, every muscle of the body should be movable independently, permitting remarkable feats of control. This ability is not an eastern prerogative. Recently, at Sydney University, anatomy lectures were illustrated by a demonstrator who could contract at will and independently every individual muscle. This man, a polio victim, had trained himself, completely restoring his health in the process.

The ability to breathe with one lung, relaxing the other, may seem an unlikely achievement, but it could be learnt in a few lessons. The method is now widely used before chest surgery, as well as for other therapeutic purposes.

The method, which is simple, could be practised in the crosslegged position or sitting in a chair.

The eyes are closed and deep and rhythmical

breathing established. With the Mind's Eye, an image of the lungs is created and the conscious thought held that both are functioning in respiration. Concentration is then moved to the right – or left – lung, and while inhaling, the image is held of *this lung only*. The existence of the other lung is completely blotted from the mind.

In the early stages concentration is only on *inhalation*. When this is mastered, complete exhalation is also practised. The student then 'changes lungs' and takes several deep breaths with both, concentrating on the thought of using them equally. *This is extremely important.*

For those in good health this technique could be regarded as just another of the many controls used in *hatha yoga*.

Heart control

One of the most important disciplines in physical yoga, achieved through the breath-mind principle, is control of the heart. A heart specialist stated recently that if this were really possible, he could see a wonderful picture of a world almost completely free of coronary occlusions.

This technique is an attempt to slow down and rest the heart. The ancient sages, aware that the longest-living animals have extremely slow heart beats, developed the method of retarding the heart through breath control and concentration.

Even if the beating rate is only slowed 2–3 beats per minute an immense amount of inner energy is saved and human life could be considerably prolonged.

Breath has a direct influence on the working of the heart. During peaceful sleep, breathing, heart rate (and bloodpressure) are much slower than during waking hours. Whenever the breath is slowed down the heart responds. When concentration is added, spectacular control could result.

During yoga training the student returns repeatedly to pacifying practice, never allowing his heart to be over-exerted. (Practices that deliberately accelerate the heart are too dangerous to give here.) *Heart-pacifying Breath* is practised either sitting with legs crossed, lying flat on the back or while walking. The breath is slowed down to 6 *Oms* (seconds or pulse-beats) for inhalation, 6 for exhalation . . . (in walking, usually 4 steps for inhalation, 4 for exhalation) . . . and a direct mental message sent to the heart to slow down.

The OM pacifying breath described on page 49 is also used in this practice.

Control of the emotions (*See also pages* 24 *and* 33)

In popular women's magazines one often sees articles which advise, in the picturesque language of the press: 'Before blowing your top at your husband, count slowly up to three.' This is sound common sense and a genuine, if unconscious, yoga practice, though no true yogi ever comes anywhere near blowing his top. In yoga it would be 3 *breaths*, though even one deep breath could have a remarkably pacifying effect.

We must never forget that *prana* is food for the nerves. A good deal of the temperamental behaviour of highly-strung, emotional people could come from nerve-starvation. Depression, lack of confidence, guilty feelings of failure or inferiority could all rise from hungry nerves or nervous centres and all could be either cured or greatly improved by the practice of deep breathing and various *prana*-accumulating methods.

Lying-down positions for breathing practice

There are four recommended lying-down positions in which to practise yoga breathing for pacifying and relaxing effect;

1. On the back, arms by sides.
2. On the stomach, face turned to one side, arms by sides.
3. On the right side, with the right arm stretched and the head resting on it, right knee drawn up; the left arm is lying loosely behind.
4. The same position on the left side.

The eyes are closed and mind concentrated on slow full rhythmical breathing, using diaphragm and stomach. These positions, which are suggested for people in poor health, even confined to bed, are also used in learning to breathe properly in sleep. Any attitude assumed during sleep is a variation of one of these four; therefore if the body has been trained to breathe correctly in these poses it will automatically continue to do so, even when unconscious. They are also an aid to overcoming insomnia. (Chinese breathing gymnastics employ the same positions, though lying on the stomach is replaced by sitting crosslegged or on a chair).

Surya Namaskar – Greeting to the Rising Sun

This is a cycle combining breathing, bending and stretching, which is said to possess great powers to tone-up and improve the whole system.

It should be practised early in the morning, at the moment of sunrise. At this time of day the air is exceptionally charged with *prana*. (It is believed that the 'marriage' of two energies takes place – energy of sun and ether (air)). Traditional practice is also accompanied by *mantra* – sounds – which heighten the benefits of inhalation-retention-exhalation.

The origin of the exercise lies in sun worship. The ancient *mantra* used are invocations to the sun; but other sounds could be substituted and the cycle has no religious significance. It is interesting, however, to compare it with the Moslem form of prayer – bending, kneeling, stretching, accompanied by cries to Allah.

An important feature of *Surya Namaskar* (page 60) is the use of full concentration and the focusing of all the mind's constructive powers upon the breathing and movements, their purpose and benefits.

The digestive system is toned-up by the bending; lungs and heart by the rhythmical deep breathing; the nervous system by the increased circulation to roots of spinal nerves and spinal cord; the figure is improved by the movements and vital energy increased by the intake and retention of *prana* in breathing.

In starting practice, do not strain or force; proceed slowly until the muscles loosen up.

1. Stand straight with feet together, hands in position of prayer.	Inhale
2. Keeping knees straight, bend down and place palms flat on the floor, if possible alongside the feet. (The hands should remain in the same position throughout the cycle.) Head is pressed to knees. (*See illustrations facing page* 32)	Exhale
3. Take a big step back with right – or left – leg into position of 'on your mark.' Head is raised to look forward.	Retain emptiness
4. Take big step back with other leg so feet are together. Knees are on the floor.	Retain emptiness
5. Raise the body, keeping it stiff, till parallel with the floor. (The arms are extended).	Inhale
6. Lower body, coming down forehead and shoulders first, keeping stiff and bending elbows as you come down.	Exhale
7. Come up into Cobra position . . . arching spine and body from the waist up, head looking up . . . pushing up against the hands. Toes are dug in.	Inhale
8. Trying not to move hands or feet, raise the buttocks so body forms triangle with the floor. The head should hang down between the arms.	Exhale
9. Take a big step forward – 'on your mark'. (This is reversing the first movements). Then big step forward with the	Inhale

other foot. The feet are now together, palms still on the floor.

10. Press head to knees; then come up into standing position with hands in position of prayer as you started. — Exhale

* There are several variations in the practice of *Surya Namaskar.* The one given here – and at our classes – is the method taught to Michael Volin by his teacher and is based on the principle of breathing in yoga *asanas.*

CHAPTER FIVE

Breathing practices – higher aspects. Strange powers acquired through breath control. Breath suspension. Levitation. The true significance of higher powers. *Pranayama. Ida* and *Pingala. Kundalini* yoga. Six *pranayamas. Chakra* Breathing. *Mudras*. Astral Breath. Higher states of consciousness. Healing breaths.

Breathing Practices. Higher aspects

Most of us, whether or not we are interested in yoga, have heard tales of fantastic feats performed by yogis who have stopped their hearts beating, suspended breath for weeks, survived burial alive for long periods, risen, even moved through the air. There are also accounts and descriptions of extraordinary rapid healings, self-administered or to others, and the existence of superhuman and psychic powers.*

Such apparent miracles are said to be brought about by complete knowledge and control of breath, and absolute mastery of concentration; but the true yogi does not exploit or display his powers for sensation or commercial gain. They are to him only steps on his path

* Early travellers wrote of '*jogis*' who lived to 350 years; who could tell future events by breathing, inflate another's body and fly 'like fowls in the air.'

towards liberation and he frowns on public exhibition. Those who do exhibit them are unworthy to possess the secrets they have learnt or stumbled upon and which in the end may destroy them.

Descriptions of some of the techniques make startling reading. A method of breath suspension, which permits burial alive, involves lengthening the tongue. This is done by gradually cutting the thin skin attaching it to the floor of the mouth. It takes about six months. A minute fraction is cut at a time – about once a week – and the slit rubbed with specially prepared powders to prevent it joining up again. The tongue is also massaged and pulled ('milked') with the fingers each day to increase its length. When it is long enough to touch the space between the eyebrows the yogi is said to be capable of practising *khechari mudra*, in which he turns the tongue back against the roof of the mouth till it blocks the entrance of the nasal passage and cuts off breath.

Khechari mudra is one of the techniques used to awaken higher faculties and its immediate purpose is, as it were, to seal up *prana* in the system. The fact that the yogi can also survive burial is incidental.

Levitation (rising into the air) is not considered an impossibility in India and Tibet. Instances have been observed and recorded and travellers have even claimed to see monks moving through space. In *Yoga over Forty* we described an island *ashram* with a stone platform projecting over a drop of 1,000 feet, from which sages were said to launch themselves into the air; and in another *ashram* where Michael Volin was a disciple, his teacher was several times described 'two feet in mid-air, legs crossed, eyes open but rolled up, slowly moving from side to side, like a balloon in a draught'.*

In the West, St. Teresa of Avila, St. Francis of Assisi and literally hundreds of other European saints were witnessed in levitation; yet the phenomenon has never been proved by scientific test. The £5,000 deposited in an English bank for such proof is still unclaimed.

Many eastern mystical schools agree with higher yoga teaching that the secret of voluntary levitation lies in breathing, combined with special *mantras* . . . combinations of sounds. Techniques involving extremely long retention build up a profound concentration of *prana* in the system, which, by effort of will, coupled with singing *mantras*, create vibrations within the body. These are directed against gravity forces, very much as little rockets attached to the belt of the modern 'bird man' enable him to soar in the air.

There is an Egyptian legend that the pyramids were built by high priests who knew this secret. By striking a rod – to create vibrations – and singing, they made the great stones rise in the air, then guided them into position with the touch of a finger. Modern mystics have suggested that the power behind 'flying saucers' is the same *prana* converted into propelling force.

Most of these higher breathing techniques involve the most subtle and complicated procedures which

* 'My teacher rarely discussed levitation and we never asked him; according to tradition, in the East, you cannot question your teacher unless he makes the first move. He never referred to his own ability to defy gravity forces and I am almost sure that he was not conscious of it.' M.V.

require the continuous personal supervision of a highly qualified teacher. Their potential dangers place them beyond the reach of ordinary students. In any case, everyone is not considered worthy of practising higher breath control, even when the specified training has been followed. The true seeker of liberation is described as 'One who is humble and chaste, speaks gently and only truth, patient, kind, has overcome anger; who has regulated his diet and abstains from intoxicating drinks and strongly seasoned food (including onions and garlic); who does not smoke hashish, tobacco or opium and who has no afflictions of heart or lungs.' In other words, higher breath control, with the psychic powers it brings, can be trusted only to those who truly merit it, physically, mentally and spiritually, and who will not exploit or misuse those powers.

There are, however, less complicated practices or *pranayamas* which could be safely learnt by any student; even, with certain reservations and care, some breathing methods that affect the mind and nervous centres.

While the simpler breathing exercises are best practised in the open, the higher methods requiring greater concentration are always done indoors . . . by tradition, never in a draught or near an open fire; never before ignorant people and, unless completely mastered, always in the presence of the *guru* or teacher.

In the East, under the strict discipline of *ashrams* or certain monasteries, breath control is still practised four times a day as prescribed by the ancient sages: dawn, midday, sunset and midnight. For the western student, twice daily, morning and evening, is enough.

Even morning practice alone could give considerable benefit.

Pranayama

Pranayama (breath control) comes fourth in the list of hatha-yoga steps . . . after *asana* or bodily poses and before mental practices.

The early yogis who studied breath control discovered that man's breathing varies during the day. At times the breath flows more freely through the right nostril, then for no apparent reason, more freely through the left . . . as though nature wished to prevent him achieving full and even control.

This theory of Dominating Nostrils is the basis of some of the most important *pranayamas* – control of *prana* through alternative nostril breathing.

Many authors identifying the word *pranayama* with the higher aspects of breath control describe it as alternative nostril breathing.* This is not strictly correct. Though it is one of the main methods there are others.

There are four actions in breath control: *Puraka* (inhalation); *recharka* (exhalation) and *kumbhaka* (retention, which is of two kinds – retention of breath and retention of emptiness).

Alternative-nostril breathing is in six parts: inhalation through the left nostril; retention; exhalation through right nostril; inhalation through right nostril; retention; exhalation through left nostril.

* The *Yoga Darshana* describes *pranayama* as 'voluntary interruptions of movements of breathing in and out.'

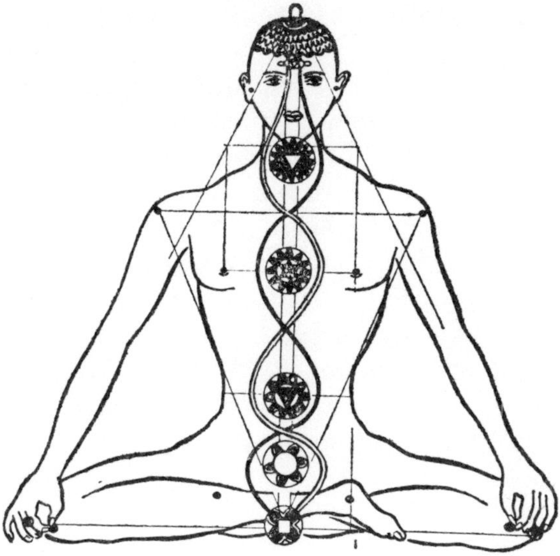

FIG. 4 Tantric anatomy – *The 7 cakras. Ida and Pingala nadis*

When *prana* is inhaled through the nose it makes first contact with the *Ida* and *Pingala nadis* in the nostrils.* (See Fig. 4). Since these nerves continue along the sides of the spine, the roots of the spinal nerves receive a completely balanced, equalized and regimented flow of life force while the breath is under control.

The mental and spiritual aspects of *pranayama* are

* In Tantric anatomy, *Ida and Pingala nadis*, (conveying positive and negative forces of *prana*) are said to originate in *Muladara cakra* (see page 79) and to cross and recross the spinal column (*sushumna*) ending in the left and right nostril respectively. Modern physiologists suggest they are the gangliated cords of the sympathetic nervous system on each side of the spine.

even more profound and extraordinary than the physical.

A branch of yoga known as *Kundalini yoga* is devoted to methods of developing latent mental and psychic powers within us. The techniques used are different breathing exercises combined with intense concentration. In the normal course of evolution these higher faculties . . . clairvoyance, telepathy, etc. . . . would take thousands of years to fully develop but through knowledge and technique the yogi could achieve them during his lifetime. He does not, however, attribute value to them in themselves, regarding them only as stages encountered in his journey of development.

Six pranayamas

As many as 36 *pranayamas* are mentioned in traditional studies but most are too complicated and involved for western students. The very prolonged retention of breath practised is dangerous unless performed under personal supervision and while special diet is observed.

The following six *pranayamas*, however, could be safely practised, often with dramatic benefits, both physical and mental.

Before practising *pranayamas* make sure that:

1. Your mind is fully receptive to the idea of conscious control of life force.

2. Your nostrils are free of impurities and perfectly clean. Purify them by a small amount of warm salt water *gently* drawn alternatively through the right nostril while the left is closed, expelling it through the

mouth. Repeat the process with the left nostril, then dry them both by rapid breathing.

3. That you will not be disturbed in any way. This is necessary for the fullest exercise of powers of concentration.

4. That the stomach is quite empty, though you should not be actually hungry.

All classical texts agree that purification of the *nadis* (nervous channels) is an extremely important preliminary to *pranayama.*

Of numerous methods the following is considered the best: Sitting in crosslegged pose (*padmasana* – lotus position – is suggested), inhale a complete breath through the *left* nostril; retain as long as comfortable, then slowly exhale through the *right.* Change nostrils and repeat a number of times.

Having made these observances, prepare a comfortable seat – a piece of one-inch thick foam rubber, a blanket folded four times etc. – and turning away from the light for a few minutes practise deep and rhythmical breathing to steady the mind.

First pranayama

This is the simplest and leads to purification of the mind.

Bend the index finger of the right hand inward, closing the right nostril with the thumb and the left with the middle finger.

Inhale through the right nostril; close it with the thumb and exhale through the left. Inhale through the left; exhale through the right. Count six heart beats for inhalation, six for exhalation.

Six *pranayamas* are suggested in the beginning, while twelve is the limit for the western student. The act of breathing is regimented in these *pranayamas* as a completely equal flow of breath through alternative nostrils.

2. *Regular pranayama*
After the flow of breath through the right and left nostril have been mastered, equally-timed retention of the breath could be practised. Sitting in Easy, Adept or Lotus position, inhale through the right nostril, keeping the left closed (6 units); retain breath also for 6 units; exhale through the left – six units; repeat the same, inhaling through the left. Three to six *pranayamas* are to be practised. Retention of the breath in this *pranayama* could be either cut by half (3 units) or increased to 12 units, providing that this is not too strenuous for the student.

3. *Classical pranayama*
This *pranayama* has a particular rhythm of inhalation, retention, exhalation, much more elaborate than the previous one.

It has been suggested in traditional yoga literature and by teachers in the East as the basis of all *Ha-tha* (sun-moon) breathing techniques involving right and left nostril.

In one of the traditional cross-legged positions, first exhale completely, then inhale through the *left* nostril counting 4 units. Then press the chin to the chest and hold the breath for 16 units. Breathe out for 8 units through the right nostril. To complete, the stomach should be drawn in as Flying Contraction (*Uddiyana*) (page 74) and retention of emptiness observed for as long as is comfortable.

The entire process is then repeated through the sun (right) nostril.

All this constitutes *one pranayama*.

The rhythm of this *pranayama* could be proportionately changed . . . instead of 4–16–8 rhythm it could be 8–32–16 or even 16–64–32. It is also permitted to retain the breath as long as comfortable.

The western student should not exceed 12 of these *pranayamas*. Up to 40 are practised daily in eastern *ashrams* under the guidance of a *guru*.

4. This *pranayama* is very simple and is known as '*surya bhedana*' (piercing of the sun).
Sitting in your favourite cross-legged position, inhale through the *right* nostril, then retain breath as long as comfortable. Exhale slowly through the same nostril. Repeat 10–20 times.

This breath control is said to 'generate bodily heat' – hence is recommended for cold weather or a cold climate – and 'cure many afflictions of the head and ensure production of bile.'

5. *Bhastrica* (Blacksmith's Bellows). (See also page 52, Chapter 4)
Sit in the Lotus position – or Easy cross-legged pose – and breathe in and out through the left nostril about 10 times. Then draw a deep breath through the same nostril and press the chin to the chest, performing

the Net-Holding Contraction (See page 74). Hold as long as possible, then breathe out through the right nostril. Release the chin and draw the stomach in (Flying Contraction, see page 74). Retain emptiness. Repeat the whole process with the right nostril.

6. *Shanmukhi mudra*. Six-faced gesture

This technique is also called 10 fingers gesture because all fingers on both hands are used.

Sitting crosslegged, inhale, through both nostrils and lock the chin to the chest. Close the ears with the thumbs, eyes with index fingers, nostrils with middle and fourth finger and put the little finger on the mouth. Retain the breath for 6–8 heart beats, then exhale slowly and release chin lock.

This technique improves mental concentration and stills the movements of the mind.

In a variation, the fourth finger is placed on the lips and the little finger is left in the air. This symbolises revitalizing the sense of touch.

Floating Breath Control

This method should be practised in the Lotus Position.

Inhale with arms raised, then lie down on the back with the hands under the neck. Retain breath as long as possible. Return to original pose and exhale.

The mind should be concentrated on the thought of extreme lightness of the body.

A similar method is to float in the water in the Fish

pose (see page 91 footnote), practising deep inhalation, retention and slow exhalation.

Mudras

The word *mudra* means to lock up or seal.

In general, the techniques known by this name involve retention of breath, creating inner pressure.

Three of the classical yoga texts – *Hathayogapradipika; Siva Samhita;* and *Gheranda Samhita* – place great importance on the practice but emphasise that since these are powerful and complicated methods they must be performed under the supervision of a teacher.

Most *mudras* – there are 25 altogether – are directly or indirectly designed to waken latent forces within.* Though impossible to describe them all in a book of this size, some of the most important are given here. (*Siva Samhita* limits its descriptions of *mudras* to 10).

Maha mudra (Arch gesture)

Sit on the floor, on a comfortable mat. Stretch the right leg and press the heel of the left foot to the *yoni* place – between anus and genitals. Lean forward, grasping the front foot with both hands. Inhale and retain the breath as long as comfortable. Practise several times, then repeat an equal number of times with the other foot.

Physically, this technique creates pressure in the head, flushing the glands and subtle nervous centres with arterial blood. It is not recommended for those with high blood pressure.

* When the 'sleeping force' (*Kundalini*) is awakened, the *sushumna* (spinal column) becomes the main road of *prana*, the mind becomes free of all connection and even death is conquered.

Jalandhara bandha (Net-holding contraction)
Although the technique is simple, this is an important *mudra.*

Sit in crosslegged position; inhale and press the chin to the chest, firmly retaining breath. Hold as long as comfortable, closing the net of the arteries of the neck (hence the name). Then, slowly exhale. The benefit is described in the traditional symbolical way: "By this contraction the wise yogi comes to drink himself the ambrosia and gains immortality".

Mula bandha (The root contraction)
Some texts pay great attention to this contraction and suggest it must accompany many of the higher breathing techniques.

It consists of powerful contraction of the anus, while breath is retained, then releasing both breath and muscles. To a certain extent it resembles *aswini-mudra* in its control of the anal muscles.

Uddiyana bandha (Flying contraction)
This technique, when done alone, consists of retention of *emptiness* – not full breath – and is unique in that respect.

It is often placed among the 7 most important hatha yoga methods leading to inner cleanliness through increased power of digestion. It may be done sitting or standing, but *only with an empty stomach* . . . at least three hours after eating a meal.

In standing position. With legs about 18 inches apart,

place the hands on the thighs with fingers towards inner part of thigh. Inhale full breath, completely exhale, then pull the stomach right in, as though to draw it against the spine. At the same time press the chin hard to the chest. Retain pressure and emptiness; then release breath and relax.

In drawing back the stomach, exert a slightly diagonal upward pull, making a hollow cave under the ribs; also lean forward, with knees slightly bent, putting weight on the palms of the hands.

In sitting position (Crosslegged, Adept or Lotus pose), the method is the same, except that hands, with fingers inward, are on the knees.

Yoga mudra

Sit in the Lotus position with hands clasped behind the back. (One hand holding the other wrist). Inhale, bend forward till head touches the floor. Retain pose and breath as long as comfortable; then exhale as you come up.

Pavanamukasana (Knees-to-stomach)

Though this is normally included among *asanas*, we give it here because it is simple to perform and has the same effects as some of the classical *mudras*.

Lie on the back, with arms by the sides. Inhale, drawing up the legs, and press the knees against the stomach with the hands, while breath is retained. Release breath and pressure and lower legs.

Since this movement flushes the head with blood it is not suitable for those with high blood pressure.

The Cakras

The *cakras* of the physical-subtle body* play a very important part in higher breathing practices, but for the western student the subject is usually one of confusion and obscurity. In traditional yoga literature they are described symbolically, sometimes with deliberate intention to confuse and mislead, for the protection of 'those in darkness' who might otherwise do themselves untold harm through wrong practice. The literal meaning of *guru* or teacher is 'one who dispels darkness'. Most *chakra* breathing must be done under direct supervision of a *guru*.

There are seven main *chakras* (wheels) or nervous-psychic centres, set one above the other (Fig. 4), each drawn in the form of a lotus with a different number of petals, each containing a different number of Sanskrit letters or characters in its centre.

Physically, the *chakras* correspond, to a certain extent, with nervous centres or nerve concentrations. By breathing methods the yogi arouses them, both on the physical and psychic plane. They react to intensified flow of *prana*, directed by concentration of thought. This is the main principle behind these practices.

The *chakras* are:

* *The Ten Vital Energies.* According to the ancient texts, there are 10 vital energies in the physical-subtle body. Each one is associated with a physical function *but is also a subtle energy.* They are listed as: *prana* – breathing; *apana* – excreting; *vyana* – circulation; *udana* – coughing; *samana* – digesting; *naga* – eructation; *kurma* – blinking; *krikara* – sneezing; *deva-datta* – yawning and *dhanam-jaya* – assimilation.

1. Muladhara (The root centre) in the base of the spine.

2. Svadhisthana (Support of Life Breath) in the genitals.

3. Manipura (Lotus of the Navel) in the solar plexus.

4. Anahata (Unstruck sound) in the middle of the chest.

5. Vishuddha (Centre of great purity) in the thyroid region.

6. Ajna (Centre of Command) between the eyebrows (The Third Eye).

7. Bramah (*Sahasrara*) (The thousand-petalled lotus) at the top of the head.

Combined breathing and concentration to arouse the *chakras* features in the awakening of higher faculties (*Kundalini* yoga) and the attainment of *samadhi* or superconsciousness, but these practices are so dangerous that they must not be attempted without personal guidance and long preparation and training. The shock to an unprepared system could cause illness, madness or death.

It is, however, permissible to practise the following *chakra* breaths:

1. *Breath to Bramah chakra* (Top of the head)

Sitting in one of the crosslegged positions, concentrate breath on the top of the head with each exhalation, imagining golden rays of *prana* penetrating your brain from within. Practise as many breaths as you feel inclined, keeping the eyes closed and body relaxed but spine and neck straight.

This practice lifts dark clouds of depression and unhappiness from the mind and brings unity with the cosmic soul.

2. *Breath to ajna chakra*

The breath is now directed to the point between the eyebrows. An image is formed of *prana* revitalizing this *chakra*, which is said to bring spiritual enlightenment, peace, balance and happiness.

3. *Breath to Vishuddha chakra*

This *chakra* corresponds with the thyroid and parathyroid glands and breath concentrated here has great physical and spiritual significance. The physical reaction is described as setting into correct balance the movements of the body's inner forces. This could be interpreted as adjustment of metabolical processes and related bodily functions.

It is said that through this practice weight could be adjusted, old age delayed, and the whole endocrinal glandular system invigorated. It is performed in crosslegged pose, through rhythmical breath and concentration. With each exhalation *prana* is directed to the *chakra*.

4. *Anahata chakra**

Some masters identify *Anahata chakra* with the cardiac plexus. Daily concentration on this *chakra* – sending not less than 12 breaths – prolongs life on the

* 'It is there that the life-breath dwells, adorned with desires, mixed with beginningless past deeds and united to the notion of I-ness.' *Siva Samhita*

physical plane. 'Auspicious results are obtained in this and other worlds', according to the *Siva Samhita.*

5. *Manipura chakra*

This may be practised sitting crosslegged or lying on the back. Place fingertips on the solar plexus and as you inhale concentrate on the thought of extra *prana* taken in, and with exhalation sent to this storage-place of energy . . . the solar plexus or *Manipura chakra.*

6. *Svadbisthana chakra*

Corresponds with the root of the penis and in traditional literature is known as 'Lord of the Water's Seed'. Concentration on this centre combined with breathing gives the yogi mastery over sexual desire and helps to open the gates of *Kundalini* power.

7. *Muladhara chakra*

To illustrate the traditional manner and language used, this is a description of *Muladhara chakra*, taken from *Siva Samhita*:

'This centre is called *kula* (the womb) and shines like gold; there is found the Self-born symbol (*Svayambhu linga*). There is found the Realized Being (Siddha) named the Double-egged (*Dviranda*). The presiding deity of this centre is *Dakini* (the Witch). In the middle of the lotus is the *yoni*, and in it lies the Coiled Energy. Above it, the shining Seed of Lust (*Kama-biga*) wanders like a flame. The wise man who ever meditates on this Root-centre, realizes the '*Darduri*' (the Frog), the Attainment which enables one to wander through space.'

Sitting crosslegged, breathing is concentrated on this *chakra* at the foot of the spine, with the mind focused upon the thought of physical inner cleanliness.

Astral Breath

In some *ashrams* and breathing schools of the East "astral breath" is regularly practised.

Teachings say that the astral body is the fluid twin of the physical and should be nourished and purified by breath. A number of maladies originate in the Astral Body, and specially trained clairvoyants could diagnose diseases which have not yet manifested in the physical plane by 'astral spectre'. In *Astral Breath*, while recharging exercises are practised, one breath is dedicated to the physical body, and one to the astral. (Purifying and pacifying breaths are similarly repeated.).

Different states of consciousness. (See note on page 93)

Better and deeper regulated breathing purifies and develops the mind.* It is absolutely essential before meditation, contemplation and self-realization for it opens the doors to super-consciousness (*samadhi*) and experience on a higher plane.

Super-consciousness cannot be fully understood until consciousness has been defined. The views of modern

* It is suggested that we use only one-fifth of our mental powers; because we do not know how to breathe correctly, four-fifths of the brain cells remain undeveloped. This possibility is now being investigated by scientists.

researchers into the human mind and different states of consciousness appear to parallel yoga teaching on this subject.

Kenneth Walker, eminent physician and philosopher, writes: 'Consciousness has often been equated with thought in western writings; but consciousness is no more thought than it is emotion, sensation or movement. It is none of our functions but is an awareness of our various activities at the moment they are occurring within us.'

The philosopher Gurdjieff described five different levels of consciousness:

1. The level of deep sleep devoid of all dreams.

2. Lighter sleep with dreams.

3. Ordinary level of consciousness, maintained during the day.

4. The state of true self-awareness, which we may seldom attain; and

5. The highest level of cosmic or universal consciousness, that is to say super-consciousness.

This corresponds very closely with yoga teachings, and while in the West attempts are made to create the state of super-consciousness by mind-opening drugs, in the East the same has been achieved for centuries by various techniques, notably breath control and meditation.

In superconsciousness 'nature holds no secrets from the yogi'. Upon entering this state, 'the closed chest containing the thousand secrets of life and death' is immediately opened.

As science advances we again find claims of the

mystics – for years rejected by the West – on the threshold of scientific confirmation. Already tests indicate the existence of a 'universal knowledge' to which individual knowledge could be tapped. Under the influence of mind-opening drugs people have spoken languages they never spoke before and described places and countries never seen in their lives.

In yoga, superconsciousness or *samadhi* is attained by techniques combining breath control and concentration; yet it can come to those who have never knowingly practised yoga. The poet Tennyson, by constant repetition of his own name (which thus acted as a mantrum), used to achieve a higher state of consciousness resembling *samadhi*; and it has been known to occur involuntarily, in young people particularly.

Involuntary *samadhi* is usually little more than a dazzling, unforgettable glimpse that comes without warning, does not last long enough to permit detailed discovery and goes as it came. Though the brief experience brings ineffable joy it remains always, in a sense, a fluke. One never knows if it will happen again; but the trained yogi has the ability to achieve it at will, to prolong it so he may more fully experience it, and to descend again, when he is ready, to the normal state of consciousness.

Those who have known *samadhi*, involuntarily or otherwise, find no difficulty in understanding why the yogi seeks to prolong it, for its revelations are accompanied by a peace, happiness and reassurance beyond normal human experience.

The techniques leading to superconsciousness are

preceded by intense and thorough purification of the body, by cleansing of the 72,000 *nadis* or nervous channels and seven *cakras* or nervous centres. The adept must observe a careful diet; his mind must be calm and undisturbed and the 'forces of soul' in balance. He chooses carefully the right time and place for practice, which is never done in the open.

In the crosslegged position, having established rhythmical breathing, he concentrates on creating a Protective Cocoon[1] . . . an invisible envelope shielding him from intrusion. The next stage is the Detachment of Perceptionary Senses,[2] a withdrawing into the Self.

The breath is then concentrated upon three different *cakras*, starting with *mulhadara cakra* (the root centre) to purify the subtle body; then upon *agna chakra* (between the eyebrows) to arouse the higher faculties of the mind; and finally upon *Brahmah cakra* (the top of the head) to open the 1,000-petalled lotus towards infinity.

The time devoted to the individual *cakras* varies according to the adept's preparedness . . . for instance, concentration upon *muladara cakra* could depend on the body's physical purity.

As each *cakra* is aroused the adept comes a stage closer to superconsciousness, culminating in an almost literal unfolding sensation in the top of the head. This traditional description of the opening of the 1,000-petalled lotus is extraordinarily similar to the experience

[1] [2] Both these techniques are practised as exercises, independent of achieving *samadhi*, and have been mastered by many western students.

of those attaining superconsciousness through mind-opening drugs.

Healing Breaths

The history of psychic healing, which includes healing by breath, is as old as mankind. Among the methods known in ancient Egypt, breathing into the nostrils was used in attempts to revive the dead. This is the same form of breath now used in the West in mouth-to-mouth resuscitation.

The basic principle of all forms of psychic healing is the transference of life force from healer to receiver.

At one stage of his training, Michael Volin was a disciple in the *ashram* of a teacher known for his powers of psychic healing. The *ashram* is described as: 'a small ancient building in a beautiful garden, surrounded by a stone wall. Green swaying branches of Chinese willows, like the sleeves of the traditional gown, dipped constantly into the waters of a little stream.

'It was a tradition for new disciples to bring a rare plant, as a graceful acknowledgement of admission to the hermitage, and now, after years of continuous growth and care it was a Garden of Eden, with every kind of shrub, tree and flower.

'Only six disciples lived here permanently. The seventh occupant was our Teacher . . . wise, kind, ageless, almost a saint; steeped in knowledge of yoga, ancient breathing gymnastics and herbs. He was a famous healer and once a week went to a nearby township to attend flocks of sufferers, always free of charge and always with great compassion.

'The touch of his small, exquisite ivory hand produced an instant sensation of physical well-being. Sometimes people were brought to the *ashram* on stretchers. Once I saw him burst into tears over the body of a young man, drowned, and dead too long to be revived.

'His teaching was that everything in the human body is in perfect balance when the balance of life force or *prana-apana* is correct. (*Apana* is a digestive power within the body. It has intentional dual meaning, referring to the union of vital breathing (*prana*) and excretory energy (*apana*)).

'He told us, "If you wish to heal you must learn how to build up a surplus of life force in your body so you could give it away without fear. You cannot exert yourself without replenishing. You cannot give without taking. You could learn to become a channel of cosmic force but only a few are capable of achieving this. To do it you must become physically pure, mentally aware, spiritually enlightened . . . These are the traditional teachings".'

The principles of healing are simple:

The first part, *accumulation*, offers considerable variety of techniques.

1. Sit down in one of the traditional crosslegged positions. Place the palms together (between knees) and interlock the fingers. Establish deep and rhythmical breathing. Close the eyes and *concentrate completely* for five minutes on the idea of building up life force. The secret of this exercise is *uninterrupted* concentration.

2. Sit as before with hands resting on the knees – thumb and index finger locked. Establish deep breathing. After each inhalation lock the breath in the chest for a few seconds; then slowly exhale, forming the image of retaining *prana*, stored in the solar plexus.

3. Lie down on your back with the legs crossed and fingers resting lightly on the solar plexus. Deeply breathe in and out, concentrating on the image of *prana* streaming through the fingertips into the body.

4. Practise *with full concentration* seven energy-charging breaths – with the solar plexus as point of concentration. Finish the cycle with three cleansing breaths and repeat the whole process twice . . . 30 breaths altogether.

5. Charge your body with energy of sun, ether, earth and water (pages 46–48).

6. Breathe deeply, imagining *prana* filling the nervous channels with each exhalation.

Before attempting healing, have a good night of sleep, eat light and nourishing food – at least three hours before treatment. You must also advise the patient to rest and above all, which is most important, infuse him with complete confidence in success.

Carefully and diligently explain the principle of breath – *pranic* healing so that there is complete rapport between you and your subject during the entire practice. Tell him or her that *prana* or universal life force, energy, is a positive power and that you are going to transfer to him some of your own life force, which could be compared with a very potent medicine, much more powerful than anything known because it is *the essence of life itself.* Your capability to convince the sufferer is more than half your success. Faith – the magic of believing – is extremely important in *pranic* healing.

Healing techniques

Healing may be done in four positions, according to the condition and nature of the ailment to be treated. The patient may be:

1. Standing erect.
2. Sitting crosslegged or on a chair.
3. Lying on the back.
4. Lying on the stomach.

Before proceeding with the treatment, feet-to-feet and hand-to-hand method is used to increase the amount of life force in the body of the patient.

Sitting on the floor, bare-foot, with knees bent, place the soles of your feet against those of the subject and lock hands with him. (See Fig. 5). For 2 or 3 minutes,

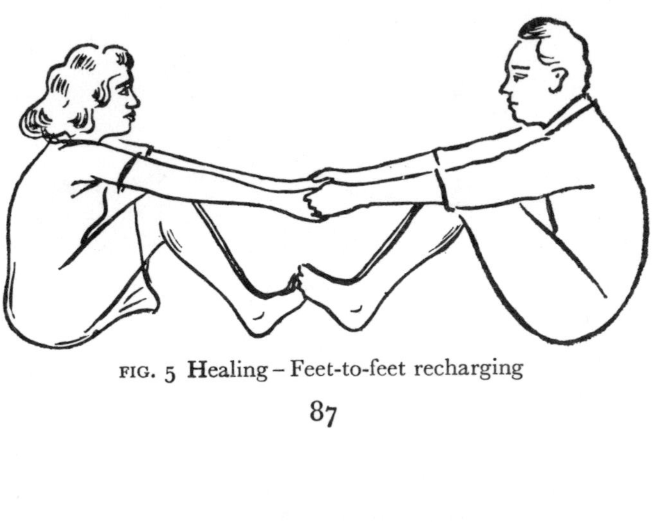

FIG. 5 Healing – Feet-to-feet recharging

keep the position, eyes closed, *both rhythmically breathing.* Advise the patient to *inhale* as you complete *exhalation* and to form an image of *your* life force drawn into his system through the hands and feet at the same time. While the patient is *exhaling* he should form an image of life force, warm, invigorating and golden in colour filling his own thousands of nervous channels.

1. *'Sweeping' the spine with prana*

With the patient lying on his stomach, arms by sides, head turned to right or left, slowly move your palms from the top of his spine down, *exhaling*, and keeping them only a few inches from his body. When you reach the base of the spine, spread the palms apart, away from the body, *inhale* and repeat the movements (see Fig. 6).

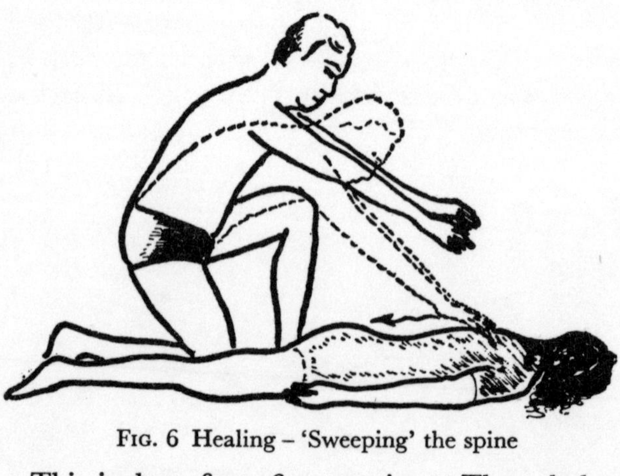

FIG. 6 Healing – 'Sweeping' the spine

This is done from 6 to 12 times. Then shake the hands as though shaking off water, place palms together and practise a recharging breath.

Before treatment, it is essential to explain the idea behind it . . . that you are invigorating the roots of the spinal nerves.

2. An even more powerful method involves actual contact with the body, when the index and first fingers are drawn upon both sides of the spine.

3. Still more potent is the clockwise movement, made with the fingers three times on each joint of the spine.

4. *Taking the malady away*

Using the right hand only, work over the affected part, bringing the palm close to it, the closing fingers as if to remove something (the malady), throw it away, forming the image of pain – affliction – removed from the patient's body. As you 'pick up' the pain, inhale and retain breath; as you throw it away, exhale. Then practise a cleansing breath.

The patient must co-operate by mentally forming the image of pain being 'taken' by your hands.

5. *Breathing prana to the affected part*

This healing method is mentioned in ancient Egyptian and Chinese books. While the principle is the same – to create a concentration of life force to break up congestion, inflammation etc. – there are considerable variations in technique.

1. Pointing finger tips to affected part, rhythmically breathing and forming image of rays of *prana* penetrating the body.

2. Gentle pressing with the fingers, while exhaling.

3. Rotary movements (always clockwise) while rhythmically breathing.

4. Vibrating movements with fingertips, breathing rhythmically.

5. Actually breathing out from distance of $1\frac{1}{2}$ feet or so, through the mouth with lips forming the letter O.

6. Bringing the lips still closer to the patient's body – 2-3 inches – so the warmth of the breath could be felt; and

7. Placing a piece of clean cotton over the affected part and actually pressing half-opened lips to the cloth, rhythmically breathing so that a sensation of pleasant warmth is soon created in the area.

This method is considered the most potent.

After all these practices the healer should rest completely (in pose of *Savasana*) and recharge himself by one of the recharging methods. Cleansing breath should always be performed at the end of the treatment.

Becoming a channel

* Much more advanced practices use the principle of the 'channel' when the Breathing Healer, after preparing himself by fasting, dieting and purification becomes an instrument, a channel of cosmic energy which he directs to the body of the sufferer.

A number of techniques are described, some of them

* Treating the limbs gently, stroke arms with downward movements from shoulders to fingertips and legs from groin to toes, always shaking the hand at the end of the movement.

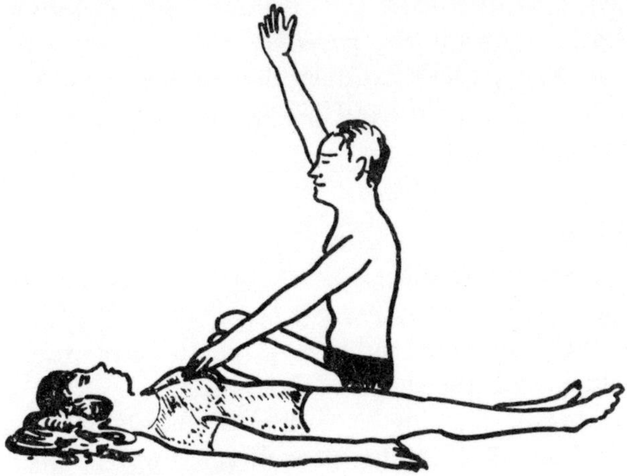

FIG. 7 Healing – Becoming a channel

remarkably similar to Chinese healing breathing gymnastics, suggesting either that the method has been adapted or springs from the same source.

1. With the patient prone on the back, the healer sits nearby with left hand resting lightly on the solar plexus (of the patient) rhythmically breathing. Sometimes the right arm is raised in the air with fingers stretched and apart as antennae, to increase the charging of *prana* from ether (Fig. 7).

2. With the patient in the Pose of a Fish* and the healer's hand on the thyroid gland.

3. The patient sits with legs stretched, holding his

* In the Fish Pose, correctly performed, the legs are locked in the Lotus position, hands rest on the toes, elbows on the ground and back is arched with head thrown back till crown rests on the floor.

toes, and the healer rests his hand on the top of his head . . . on the *Brahmah Chakra*.

4. The patient assumes the Supine Pelvic* pose with the healer's hand on the centre of the chest (cardiac plexus).

Distant healing

Prana, Essence of Life, is not entirely a physical force. It is also governed by psychic laws.

It could be sent through space, to any distance, travelling with the speed of thought.

In Distant Healing, it is first accumulated by the physical act of breathing, then directed to its object by power of concentration. This may be done with or without the knowledge of the receiver.

The sender sits in the crosslegged pose and after establishing deep breath evokes the image of the receiver, with each exhalation imagining the channel of *prana* streaming to the receiver's solar plexus. These streams of life force could be directed to any part of the body, the 'sweeping' or penetrating action being imagined by the sender.

Since it is believed that greater benefits are obtained with the conscious co-operation of the receiver, it is best to arrange an exact time for the practice. Distance is no object.

After Distant Healing the sender must always

* To perform Supine Pelvic pose, sit back on the heels, or split heels and sit on the floor between them with legs at the sides; arch the spine and come back till crown of the head rests on the floor. Hands are in position of prayer in area of solar plexus.

perform Cleansing Breaths and completely rest and relax.

Self-healing

In self-healing, the body must also be first charged with vital energy before it is directed to the part to be healed.

Lie down with legs crossed (knees drawn up and apart) and fingertips lightly touching the solar plexus. Concentrate for a few minutes on accumulating *prana*; then sit upright and continue the deep breathing while directing the accumulated *prana* to the seat of affliction.

Note

Higher states of consciousness

Experiences in states of heightened consciousness, whether involuntary or induced by drugs, often include realization or awareness of conditions or practices described in yoga teaching, though the 'discoverer' knows nothing of yoga.

Instances described – both verbal and printed – include: *Awareness that every part of the body has a separate and individual life;* that each organ could be spoken to or directed. (cf. yoga teaching that every cell in the body has its own instinctive mind, which takes orders from the master mind in the brain; also the yoga exercise, *Conversation with Vital Organs*, based on belief that each organ could be spoken to and directed or encouraged).

Recognition of the connection between breathing and higher states of consciousness . . . that breath control is the key to entering these higher states . . . that there is a definite (involuntary) change in breathing at the approach of the trance-like state. Realization of the immense power of breath – far beyond normal physical functions.

The experience of a physical 'force' moving up the spine – (cf. Yoga teaching that *Kundalini* (latent energy) moves up *sushumna* (the central column) – rousing the *cakras* and bringing higher state of consciousness).

The true and actual knowledge and understanding of the dangers in too great revelations to a body and mind unprepared to receive them – (cf. Yoga teaching that intense preparation and purification must precede higher breathing practices).

Other coinciding experiences include – a sense of separation from the physical body; the sense of *being* sound, colour; the appearance of a brilliant white light; the sense of seeing all creation from an immense height; of absolute identification with all creation and complete assurance, peace and joy. All these are experienced by the yogi in the state of *samadhi* induced by breath control.

Superconsciousness achieved by drugs, however, is said to bring no lasting sense of spiritual illumination, and is therefore of little value to the true seeker, apart from the dangers of the practice.

The same procedure is followed sitting in crosslegged position.

These Indian yoga Cleansing Breaths may be supplemented by a standing breath taken from the ancient Chinese breathing gymnastics, which are believed to have developed from yoga.

In the Chinese method the Standing Cleansing Breath is accompanied by vigorous rubbing of the lower ribs and tapping the chest during exhalation, to expedite discharge of stale air.

Bhastrica (Blacksmith's Bellows)

This is a powerful purifying breath which is known as the 'bloodstream purifier'. The name suggests the technique, in which oxygen is literally pumped into the blood as the blacksmith blows air into his fire with the bellows. As the air makes the fire burn brighter, it purifies and speeds up the blood circulation carrying oxygen to the body cells.

Sit cross-legged. Breathe in and out quickly through the nose about ten times, by which time you will have the feeling of panting, as though after rapid exertion. Then draw in a deep breath and exhale through the mouth with lips forming an O, blowing out the air in sharp blasts.

Repeat once or twice more.

It is not advisable to practice more than three times (30 breaths in all), and where there is any cardiac or chest condition that forbids acceleration of heart or breathing the exercise must not be attempted.

Bhastrica could also be practised by inhaling and